A STEP BY STEP BOOK ABOUT
SETTING UP
AN AQUARIUM

DR. CLIFF W. EMMENS

Photography: D. Fesver, A. Roth, Burkhard Kahl, Hans-Joachin Richter, Dr. Harvy Grier, Dr. Warren E. Burgess, R. Zukel, Michael Gilroy, Edward C. Taylor, I. Kadlec.

Humorous illustrations by Andrew Prendimano.

Distributed in the UNITED STATES by T.F.H. Publications, Inc., One T.F.H. Plaza, Neptune City, NJ 07753; in CANADA to the Pet Trade by H & L Pet Supplies Inc., 27 Kingston Crescent, Kitchener, Ontario N2B 2T6; Rolf C. Hagen Ltd., 3225 Sartelon Street, Montreal 382 Quebec; in CANADA to the Book Trade by Macmillan of Canada (A Division of Canada Publishing Corporation), 164 Commander Boulevard, Agincourt, Ontario M1S 3C7; in ENGLAND by T.F.H. Publications Limited, Cliveden House/Priors Way/Bray, Maidenhead, Berkshire SL6 2HP, England; in AUSTRALIA AND THE SOUTH PACIFIC by T.F.H. (Australia) Pty. Ltd., Box 149, Brookvale 2100 N.S.W., Australia; in NEW ZEALAND by Ross Haines & Son, Ltd., 18 Monmouth Street, Grey Lynn, Auckland 2, New Zealand; in the PHILIPPINES by Bio-Research, 5 Lippay Street, San Lorenzo Village, Makati Rizal; in SOUTH AFRICA by Multipet Pty. Ltd., 30 Turners Avenue, Durban 4001. Published by T.F.H. Publications, Inc. Manufactured in the United States of America by T.F.H. Publications, Inc.

Contents

AQUARIA

Fish-keeping is a very ancient hobby in the western world, going back at least as far as early Rome and, in the Far East, probably further. Fishes were kept either for consumption or for pleasure, but in any case were housed in containers allowing a view only from the top, as in a pond. Glass was made by the Egyptians in 1500 B.C., but no large vessels appear to have been available. The first accounts of fishes being kept in glass bowls date from around 1600 A.D. The Chinese used porcelain bowls of considerable translucency and were seemingly uninterested in glass vessels when they were first brought in from Europe.

No precise dates are available for the introduction of rectangular or polygonal glass aquaria, but it was probably not until the early or mid-19th century. A British naturalist, P. H. Gosse, coined the word "aquarium" in 1853 and published a book entitled *The Aquarium* in 1854. Many other publications followed in Europe, particularly in Germany and Britain. Their authors were using large glass bowls, rectangular or hexagonal tanks, many of which were *vivaria* rather than *aquaria*—meaning that they housed decorative plants above the water and often had little fountains operated from a reservoir. The fishes were native or goldfish, often accompanied by newts or salamanders.

These early aquaria were unheated, unlit except naturally, and without aeration other than from the fountain if present. Around the close of the 19th century, preference for rectangular tanks, often with only a glass front, was becoming established and the books then published usually included in-

structions for making and furnishing them. They would usually be furnished with a mud or sand bottom into which plants were set with decorative rocks and stones often included.

Heat and aeration in the aquarium were effected early in the 20th century in Germany and the U.S.A., usually by oil burners or hot pipes beneath the tanks and by various types of pumps and air releases. The upsurge of tropical fish-keeping had begun. Artificial lighting lagged behind and it was generally believed that strong light was detrimental. In 1925, for instance, E. C. Boulenger, director of the London Zoo's aquarium, wrote, "Nearly all the fish diseases and other troubles which exasperate the aquarist are caused, if not by sudden changes of temperature, by too much light." Views changed during the next decade or so, and by the middle of the century, electric top lighting was commonly employed.

THE MODERN AQUARIUM

Today's aquarium is made of plate glass cemented together with silicone rubber (a resilient, clear preparation that never sets hard but is immensely strong and needs no support-

Early aquariums relied solely on the water surface area to provide a supply of oxygen to the fishes. Because this method of oxygenation is less efficient than today's use of pumps and filters, it was necessary to house many fewer fishes in the early aquariums.

The use of air-stones allows us to oxygenate our tanks to a great degree and therefore keep healthy fishes without the worry of suffocation.

ing frame). A so-called "high" tank looks better than the double-cube that used to be popular. For the beginning aquarist, a tank between 24" x 15" x 12" (60 cm x 37½ cm x 30 cm) and 36" x 18" x 15" (90 cm x 45 cm x 37½ cm) is about right. The length is given first, then the height and width, and the dimensions quoted would hold 18 and 42 gallons (68 and 160 liters) if filled only with water.

Tanks within this range are inexpensive but are large enough to give a good display of plants and fishes. They will weigh around 250 to 500 lb (114 to 228 kg) and thus need good support, but they are not too heavy to be placed on conventional furniture stands if you wish. They should be made of ¼" plate (6 mm glass) with preferably a ⅜" plate base (9 mm glass). Careful support is needed, on a flat, even surface such as a sheet of styrofoam that will take up any slight irregularities. Make sure that whatever you choose is waterproof and do not use cardboard or anything similar that eventually will become damp and troublesome.

The tank will have cover glasses to keep splashes and fishes inside and prevent unwanted materials from entering. These should sit on countersunk supports so that water cannot run over the outside. The cover glasses should have handles and should allow for the passage of heater cables and air lines and for a small segment to be removed for feeding. They need not be as thick as the rest of the aquarium, but must not be thin enough to get broken easily. The aquarium light or lights will sit over the cover glasses in a hood of some sort, protected from above and below.

Buying a complete tank set-up can often save the aquarist money, because pet stores will often offer complete tank set-ups at bargain prices. It is often stated and frequently ignored, when buying a tank, especially your first, buy the largest tank that you can afford, house, and care for. Once you are an established aquarist, you will understand and appreciate this statement.

A heater is necessary for any tropical tank; they are safe, simple to install, and mostly inexpensive. Heaters come in different degrees of power; choose one that is appropriate for your specific tank, as too powerful a heater can cook your fishes if you are not careful. A heater with a built-in thermostat is best.

HEATING

A heater, controlled by a thermostat that is usually built into it, will be needed in the tropical tank. It may be totally submersible or have its top, with controls, sitting out of the water. In the first case, it will usually be placed horizontally on the gravel; in the second, it must necessarily be placed upright. For this reason, and because it can be hidden more easily, I prefer the submersible type. If you start to give a partial water change and forget to turn off the heater, no harm is done if the heater remains below water level, whereas an upright heater may shatter or short. The heater will normally have a pilot light that tells you when it is functioning; but, if the light stays on and the tank is still cooling down, the heater has failed.

Choose a heater that is adequate for its purpose and no more. Too powerful an instrument can cook your fishes if it stays on by accident. A heater capable of keeping the aquarium temperature about 20°F (11°C) above room temperature is adequate except in unheated rooms in cold climates. For a 15 gallon aquarium, a 75 watt heater is ample, and for a 30 gallon aquarium, 150 watts.

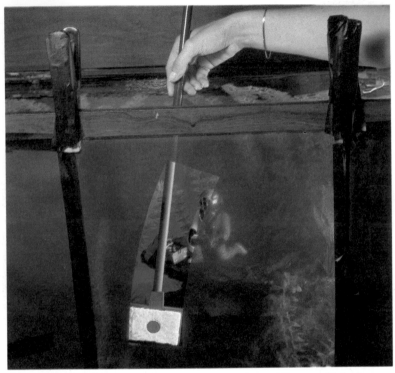

An aquarium that is well lighted and kept warm (70-80°F) is very likely to accumulate algae. Such fishes as"plecko-"catfish and algae-eaters and many snails will help to keep such algae growth under control, yet it is still a good idea to have an algae-scraper such as shown above to keep your glass clean.

A thermometer will also be needed. Don't use a mercury one, because if it breaks it can poison the water. A floating or stick-on alcohol thermometer is satisfactory; so is the liquid crystal type that is stuck onto the outside of the tank. This type may read a degree or two low in a cool room, but you can allow for that if greater accuracy is needed—which is rarely the case. The average tropical tank is kept at 73°–77°F (23°–25°C) and should not wander over a greater range for fear of harming the fishes. Sometimes a tank will be kept at a different range, say 80°–84°F (27°–29°C) but there should be a justifiable reason for this.

Aquaria

LIGHTING

The standard lighting for modern aquaria is fluorescent. It is cool and gives more light per watt than incandescent bulbs. It is also available in many different varieties that offer the aquarist a choice of spectral ranges and intensities. If plants are to be cultivated, the two ends of the visible spectrum should be present in adequate amounts; but, tubes deficient in the central region look purple (blue + red) and may not suit their owner. On the other hand, they might, as such tubes tend to enhance the colors of the fishes.

If you wish to cultivate living plants, it may be necessary to purchase an aquarium bulb designed specifically for this purpose. It helps to make this decision prior to purchasing your set-up; that way you can acquire the proper bulb at the start and not get stuck with one not appropriate for your purposes.

White, daylight, or "natural" lighting is adequate for plants and gives a more normal look. There are also special fluorescents made for aquaria that combine the best of both worlds. Take a good look at what is available before you decide what suits your own taste and the needs of your plants. The fishes don't mind as long as they can see well enough to swim around and feed.

Lush plant growth is very attractive and gives the aquarium a look of natural beauty. Plants also help to keep the aquarium clean by feeding on tank sediment; they also produce oxygen during their photosynthesis phase.

A single tube running the full length of the aquarium is fairly standard for freshwater tanks, but better plant growth and a wider choice of illumination can be had by two or even more tubes. For instance, one daylight and one good plant stimulating tube can give a very acceptable look to the aquascape and stimulate very good plant development. Be careful about your choice and don't over-illuminate fishes coming from shaded waters or they will hide away all the time. Standard plant light tubes are weaker than most others and are very suitable for such fishes. Special incandescent tubular showcase bulbs are usually available at most pet shops.

With a single tube, keep the light on for at least 12 hours per day; longer is quite O.K. Don't switch it on suddenly in a dark room. Either put the room lights on first or use a dimmer-switch. Similarly, don't plunge the fishes suddenly into darkness or they may panic and be unable to locate their usual resting places. Keep the room lights on for a few minutes at least after switching off the tank lights.

AERATION

The surface of the water is where the normal aquarium "breathes." If it is left undisturbed, less exchange of gases will occur and the lower regions of the tank may become deficient in oxygen.

Actually, as the older aquarists know, it is rarely necessary to aerate a freshwater tank that is not overstocked or overheated; aeration is a rather pretty way of taking out insurance. It is the turnover of water that matters, as the rising bubbles

Air-pumps come in a variety of sizes and strengths; purchase one that best fits your needs.

draw a column of water with them and constantly renew the water surface. The exchange between the water and the bubbles themselves is of minor significance unless aeration is very brisk indeed. The heater also causes rising water currents and so helps in the surface interchange, that is, the release of carbon dioxide and uptake of oxygen.

Airstones that release the bubbles are made of various materials—fused ceramic granules most commonly. They should give a fairly fine but not too fine stream of bubbles, with

A single pump can supply several air-stones or other air-fixtures if used in conjunction with an adapter such as shown above. These are very easy to install and allow for a creative use of air-fixtures.

an average diameter around $\frac{1}{40}''$ (0.5 mm). Wooden air releases give very fine bubbles and work better in air-lifts than for general aeration. They also tend to clog up rather quickly. All airstones need periodic cleaning if they are to function to best advantage. A dunk in hot water and a good brushing will usually suffice.

Air pumps to supply the air to the airstones via plastic tubing are of many varieties; but, the cheapest and potentially

quietest, also quite sufficient for all normal purposes, are diaphragm pumps. It is difficult in a petshop to hear just how quiet
a particular pump is, so arrange to have it exchanged if it
proves too noisy. A really quiet pump cannot be heard if you
place it in a nearby cupboard. It may gradually get noisier as
time passes; this indicates that a new diaphragm should be fit-
ted, a simple procedure.

When you buy your pump, also purchase a set of
gang-valves to service several airlines (to airstones, filter, etc.)
and a non-return valve that allows you to place the pump below the level of the water without fear of water syphoning
back. A variable output control is an advantage also, and is fit-
ted to many models. Buy plenty of soft plastic tubing as well,
enough to service everything you are likely to install plus some
extras.

FILTERS

Just as with aeration, a filter is not necessary in a well-
serviced freshwater aquarium, but it helps a lot and saves you
work. Many of our present day items of equipment are time-
savers and insurances against neglect or mistakes of one kind
or another. There are different types of filters.

A filter is considered standard equipment by today's hobbyists; filters allow you
to safely house more fishes per tank than would otherwise be allowed. Pictured
below is *Hemigrammus pulcher*.

MECHANICAL FILTERS are designed to remove particles from the water by passing it through a medium such as plastic matting that traps most of the floating material. Very fine filter media may be used in so-called power filters which trap even algae and bacteria by forcing the water through a capsule with microscopic pores.

CHEMICAL FILTERS purify the water by taking up dissolved materials such as toxins and colored matter. Activated charcoal or carbon does this very effectively, but only if in fine, dull-looking granular form that is sandwiched between layers of plastic matting and so combines mechanical and chemical filtration in one. Other filter materials may be used to absorb ammonia or to correct pH.

Shown here is the return tube of an undergravel filter; such filters are biological filters and are highly recommended. In the container at the top of the tube can be placed ammonia-removing tablets, thus combining chemical and biological filtration.

For a small, freshwater aquarium, a power filter may be all that is required; These often combine mechanical and chemical filtration.

BIOLOGICAL FILTERS make use of bacteria that grow on the filter medium and convert waste materials to harmless ones. The most important of these convert ammonia, the end result of the breakdown of nitrogen-containing substances, to nitrates. These bacteria are slow-growing but will eventually collect on virtually any filter material; however, mechanical filters are usually changed too often for them to have much effect biologically. Biological filtration is so important that we shall discuss it separately.

There are very many different types of filters and nearly all of them do an efficient job, but for the ordinary aquarium a very simple set-up is all that is needed. It may be placed inside the aquarium or hung outside it. There are two kinds of inside filters and one outside filter to be recommended:

1. A plastic ¼-cylinder that sits in a back corner of the tank, hidden by plants or rocks. Water flows into it via a perforated lid, through a sandwich of filter mats and activated carbon, and is then lifted up through a central tube by bubbles released from an airstone or even by a crude jet of coarse bubbles. The filter is thus an aerator as well and works

A filter that is hung over the side of the tank allows you to change or clean the filter with minimal disruption to your aquarium.

    nicely for tanks up to about 20 gallons (76 liters).

2. For larger tanks, a filter hung or held by suction cups at the top of the tank so as to project just above the water level is more suitable. An airlift pumps water into the top of the filter, and it then flows down via a sandwich as in type 1, out through a perforated base. The airlift is simply a plastic tube hung from the side of the filter and a flow of air into its base carries water over. The intake is protected by a perforated guard to prevent anything large being sucked in.

3. A filter with a solid base may hang outside the aquarium, and in that case it must have an arrangement for a return of water to the aquarium. This is usually the "active" part of the filter and consists of any airlift (or pump in more sophisticated models) returning water to the tank. The intake or intakes are simply syphons with guards and carry water passively into the filter. This arrangement prevents accidental pumping of water out of the tank should the return from the filter become blocked.

THE BIOLOGICAL FILTER

Biological filters must have a large surface area on which the necessary bacteria may grow. There are various designs for filters outside the aquarium, but we shall confine ourselves to the original undergravel filter, ample in capacity for the freshwater tank. It uses the gravel itself as a filter medium and consists of a plastic plate with many narrow slots and supported about ½″ (1 cm approx.) above the base of the aquarium. An airlift at one corner, or several in a large aquarium, raises water from under the plate and so draws water down

Because there are so many different filters, and indeed almost all aquarium products, it is wise to get the advice of your local pet store owner concerning the right filter, or other product, for you.

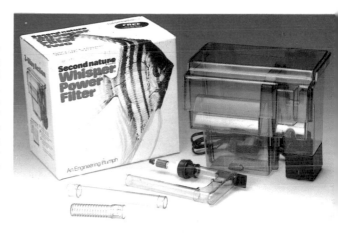

through the gravel, in which the bacteria proliferate.

The gravel over the plate should be unable to penetrate it, so if the slots are, say, ½₅″ (1 mm) in diameter, the gravel must be larger, but not too large, so as to give as great a total area as possible. A depth of 2–3″ (5–7½ cm) and an average grain size of ½₁₂″ (2 mm) is about right. If in any doubt, put a layer of plastic flyscreen over the filter plate. Some aquarists find that not all plants flourish if over such a filter, although others deny this. However, there is no need for the filter to cover the whole base and a very satisfactory arrangement is to place a relatively small filter plate with its airlift at center back and the plate as a diamond with a point near center front. Unless you want a plant as a centerpiece, the open area above the plate is normally left unplanted.

The combination of an undergravel filter and a carbon filter gives just about ideal filtration. The undergravel filter removes nitrogenous toxins, and the carbon filter other toxins, plus yellow color that otherwise develops despite partial water changes. Even the partial undergravel filter recommended has a considerable capacity for purifying the water and is a great insurance against pollution.

GRAVEL, ROCKS

Gravel is excellent for plants, with or without an undergravel filter. Its nature is very important and, for a tank of neutral pH, alkaline substances such as coral sand, shell-grit or dolomite are absolute no-nos. Silica sand, coarse river sand, crushed granite or any other neutral material may be used after a very thorough washing. Your local petshop will have the best material available in your area.

Gravel comes in many shapes, sizes, and colors. Some form of gravel is recommended for almost every aquarium; yet many fishes require a specific type. Know your fish and find out what is the best gravel for your tank.

Fish do best if kept in an environment that closely resembles their natural habitat. Pictured is *Serrasalmus nattereri*.

The same applies to any rockwork you may choose to include, so that marble, sea-shells, coral or any alkaline rock must be avoided. Driftwood may make for a very attractive aquascape, especially for fishes from areas where tree roots or fallen branches are found. Give it a good soak in fresh water first. There are those who like to see mermaids and wrecks, or frogs that open their mouths to let air bubbles out.

OTHER EQUIPMENT

Don't forget that you will need such things as a syphon, a net or nets, and a pH test kit in addition to those items already listed. Despite modern gadgetry, the best syphon is a length of rubber tubing attached to a glass or a rigid plastic tube a little longer than the depth of the tank. If you use glass tubing, tip it with an inch or so of rubber to prevent chipping or cracking it. Rubber tubing about ½″ (1 cm) in diameter is easy to control.

You may decide to buy a water changer; that certainly helps in keeping a clear and healthy tank, but remember to calibrate it so that you know how much water is removed, and that it does not remove mulm (the debris that collects on the bottom). This must be syphoned off periodically.

There is an art to setting up an aquarium. Some of us can do it automatically, but unless you have had considerable practice, it pays to follow a series of preplanned steps along the lines suggested here.

SETTING UP

1. Make a sketch or two of how you want the tank to look—from the top and from the front. Include the filter, heater, etc., in your planning and calculate the number of rocks, plants, and other decorations you need. Think about the fishes you intend to house and see that the layout suits them. Don't just buy plants and then fishes at random. I know that you will do it to some extent, but try from the beginning to make things compatible: tall, strap-like plants predominating with angelfishes, nice thickets of other plants for danios or top minnows to inhabit, and so on.

2. Wash the gravel thoroughly; it may need a dozen successive washings portion by portion in a bucket of water with thorough hosing until the water runs clear. Failure to do this can result in cloudy water that is difficult to clean up. Disinfect rocks and plants by leaving them for 24 hours in ⅕ grain of potassium permanganate per gallon (3 mg per liter), or for 15 minutes in ½ grain per gallon (7.5 mg per liter), followed by a wash in tap water. Wash out the aquarium thoroughly with tap water and clean all glass surfaces. Never use any ordinary household disinfectant for these jobs; it can cause endless troubles, the least of which may be a persistent odor. Instead, use one of the disinfectant products made specifically for use with aquariums.

3. Prepare the site for the aquarium. Make sure that it is absolutely level and then tape the styrofoam sheets or

FACING PAGE: This is a well planted, well planned aquarium; experienced hobbyists recommend that you plan your aquarium on paper before actually setting it up. Among the species most prominent here are angelfish, bleeding heart tetras and hatchetfish.

An unfilled aquarium is rather light. If you are setting up alone or if you are working with a large aquarium, it is recommended that you set your tank in place prior to filling it, as this may save a heartbreaking experience. Also, be sure that your initial aquarium site will be suitable for some time to come.

whatever you have chosen into position temporarily. They will shift if you don't! With any but the smallest tank, two people should lower it carefully into position, holding it by the base, not the top. See how good you are at getting fingers out of the way! Then check that you cannot slip a knife blade between the tank and the styrofoam anywhere. If you can, start again and get things really level.

4. If you are installing an undergravel filter, which I strongly recommend, place it in position, leaving a small space between it and the front of the aquarium so that it will not be visible when the gravel is added. With or without the filter, place the wet gravel in position with a scoop of some kind so as to form a shallow ½-basin with its low point at center front. It should slope from 3–4" (7½–10 cm) at the back to at least 2" (5 cm) at its low point. Not only does this arrangement look better than a flat surface, but it helps mulm to collect where it is easily removed.

5. Now place all equipment and decoration in position, anchoring leads and airlines with them or with small

stones so that they stay put as the tank is filled with water. Take care that the heater is free of contact with the aquarium glass and cannot easily become buried. Nobody seems to have invented rests for fully submersible bottom heaters, but they should.

6. Place a small basin or similar vessel at center front and run a hose into it, after having previously run the water for at least a few minutes to clear the pipes of stagnant and possibly polluted water. Then turn on the water very gently so that it flows over into the aquarium with minimal disturbance. If the use of a hose is impossible, a watering can or jug can be substituted. Fill the tank half-way—no more.

7. Trim the roots of your plants to a mere 1–2″ (2½–5 cm) to make planting easy. Place the roots of each plant along your forefinger and push them under the gravel from a position

When filling your aquarium, it is helpful if you place a dish, or other object capable of displacing the flow of water, on the gravel at the bottom of the tank. When filling, it is best to proceed at a moderate rate, keeping an eye out for cracks or other faults that may create complications in the future.

a few inches away from the desired position. They will then finish up where you want them. Take care not to bury the crowns of any plants like *Sagittaria* or Amazon swords. Smooth out the gravel.

As a general guide, place tall plants at the back and sides of the aquarium and short ones toward the front, leaving the center bare. A tallish plant may, however, act as a centerpiece. For a nice planting, reckon on at least one plant per gallon. When the tank is full, any disturbance of your arrangements can best be corrected using planting sticks—a pair of narrow sticks with a **V**-notch at one end. These can be purchased from your dealer.

8. Although optional at this stage, it is an advantage

Before the purchase and set-up of your new aquarium, it really pays to have a good idea of the purpose for which you plan to use your aquarium; with so many starter packages and specialized kits available, knowledge of intention will help make decisions more simple.

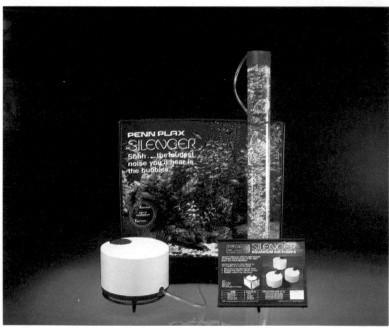

The first fishes to be introduced into your newly established aquarium should be few in number, hardy, and inexpensive.

to add a starter preparation that inoculates the tank with the bacteria needed for the nitrogen cycle and that converts ammonia to nitrates. Alternatively, you can add some gravel from a disease-free tank or a few pinches of garden soil containing the same bacteria. This ensures a rapid development of the biological filter, if present, and increases the activity of the gravel even if it isn't.

9. The aquarium can now be left for a day, just in case of a leak (unlikely as it may be), or you can go straight ahead and fill it up. It will look best if the water comes right up to the cover glass supports so that no water line is seen. Put the cover glasses in position and switch everything on and leave it for several days, during which you can check that all is well—temperature around 75°F (24°C), pH around 7.0, all equipment working. If your local water is heavily chlorinated, don't worry, it will all blow off; but if it has chloramines in it (combinations of ammonia and chlorine), these are not so easily disposed of

27

and must be neutralized with a commercial preparation or with 1 gram per gallon (15 mg per liter) of sodium thiosulphate (photographer's "hypo"). If necessary, adjust the pH with a commercial kit, or add about a level teaspoon (5 ml) per 40 gallons (152 liters) of sodium bicarbonate step by step to increase it and of sodium acid phosphate to decrease it. Use a standard 5 ml teaspoon rather than any old spoon; they are easy to purchase, usually in sets of ¼, ½, 1 and 2 plastic teaspoons.

10. The plants and undergravel filter will take a few weeks to settle down and function properly, but they do best if a few fishes are added after the first few days. These are prefer-

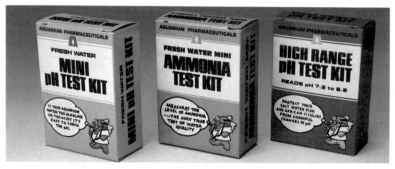

If you decide to mature your tank by using ammonium chloride, the purchase of an ammonia test kit will be required.

ably hardy species like livebearers, barbs, danios, catfishes or loaches. Add only about a quarter of the number the aquarium can theoretically hold. Then add similar numbers at weekly intervals until the aquarium is fully stocked, leaving the tenderest until last.

11. There is an alternative if it is necessary to stock the tank in one operation. Instead of maturing it with live fishes, use ammonium chloride. This will require the purchase of a nitrite kit and a 10% solution of the ammonium salt. Add 2 ml per day per 25 gallons (100 liters) for the first two days, then 4 ml per day for the next two days and so on until 10 ml per day is reached. Start measuring the nitrite concentration on day 10 and repeat it every other day. It will rise to perhaps 10

Guppies, even the more fancy breeds, are hardy fishes that can be among those first introduced into your tank.

ppm (parts per million or mg per liter) and then fall again after several weeks. When it falls to below 0.5 ppm, stop adding ammonia and put the fishes in on the next day. If there is no undergravel filter, halve the ammonium chloride added per day and expect a wait of one to two months. All very tedious, but worth the trouble.

FISH CAPACITY

The number of fishes an aquarium can safely hold depends on their size, type, and on the surface area of the tank. Aeration can double this capacity, but it is best to regard it as an insurance and not to depend on it to keep the fishes healthy. In addition, freshwater tropicals can be crowded and go on living but in most cases they would look too concentrated, as they often do in the petshop tanks. An approximate surface area requirement for various sizes of fish, ignoring the tail fin, is as follows; some fishes require more or less crowding than others. Discuss it with your petshop owner.

BODY LENGTH		NO. PER SQ. FT OF WATER SURFACE (900 sq cm)	AREA PER FISH	
In	Cm		Sq in	Sq cm
1	2.5	55	2.6	16.8
1½	3.8	20	6.6	42.6
2	5.1	12	12.5	80.6
2½	6.4	7	20	129
3	7.6	5	30	194
4	10.2	2	65	419
5	12.7	1	120	774
6	15.2	1	180	1161

These calculations are much better than "inches per gallon," because a 2" fish has eight times the body weight (biomass) of a 1" fish and requires approximately eight times the oxygen, not twice as the inch-per-gallon-rule suggests. Although some fishes are slim and others fat, the slimmer and lighter fish is usually more active and tends to consume much the same amount of oxygen as the bulky one. There is an exception to the rule, however, with fishes that have a labyrinth, like gouramis, and breathe air. These need only half the water surface indicated.

The average length of the fishes you buy will probably be about 2" (5 cm), and so as a very rough guide you can expect a 24" (60 cm) fifteen gallon tank to hold about 24 fishes and a 36" (90 cm) thirty gallon tank to hold about twice that number. This allows for some growth and could be cautiously exceeded with good aeration and maintenance.

INTRODUCING FISHES

Never plunge a new fish straight into your aquarium. Why not? Because it may be seriously stressed by changes in water quality, such as pH, temperature and hardness. It may be set upon by the other fishes and, in extreme cases, be killed or

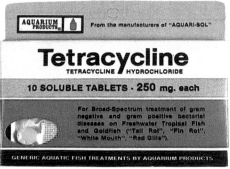

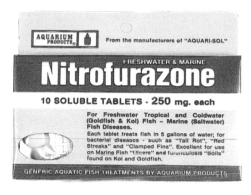

Most seasoned aquarists will recommend a quarantine period for any newly purchased fishes. During this time, the job of the hobbyist is to keep a close lookout for any symptoms of disease, and, if necessary, to treat the affected fish with the proper medication.

The fishes that you bring home from the pet store will most probably be contained in small plastic bags. Take time to acclimate your new fishes and test the water both in the bag and in your tank; make the necessary adjustments over a period of time—not all at once. Remember that the air supply in the bag is limited, even to labyrinth fishes such as *Betta macrostoma*.

be so intimidated as to hide away and starve. Find out what the temperature of the fish's original tank was and if possible its pH. Your dealer should know. The more they differ from your own tank, the slower should be the introductory period.

Although we should do so, few of us quarantine freshwater fishes before introducing them to the display tank—mainly because few of us maintain the necessary facilities. But we can take all reasonable precautions. I live in a country where all imported freshwater fishes must, by law, be quarantined under strict conditions before sale and so it is reasonably safe to introduce them to the display tank immediately. If you are not so lucky, ask your dealer how long he has had a particular fish, if it has been treated for disease prior to sale and, of course, use your own eyes to check carefully the condition of the fish. As long as you don't do it too often, treat the whole tank with a safe disinfectant if you are suspicious of any newcomer. Acriflavine (Trypaflavine) or Monacrin (monaminoacridine) are such, and will help to guard against the most common undetected pest—velvet disease. Use a stock solution of 0.2% and add one teaspoon (5 ml) per 5 gallons (20 liters). There are commercial preparations that can be used instead, containing not only such a chemical but others in combination with it.

Back to putting fishes into aquaria! Your new fishes will be packed in plastic bags that, if placed in an insulated container, should remain at a reasonable temperature unless on a very long journey. Measure temperature and pH on arrival; if they do not differ from those of your tank by more than 3°F (1.5°C) hotter or 5°F (3°C) cooler or by 1 pH unit, take at least a half hour over the following procedure. If they do differ more in either temperature or pH, take up to several hours.

Float each bag in the aquarium, open it up, and start to change the water. Use a baster or large syringe to remove about one-third of the water and replace it with water from the

Treatment in a quarantine tank can include the use of an anti-bacterial agent and/or other chemical preparations. These can also be used in your community tank, but discretion must be used.

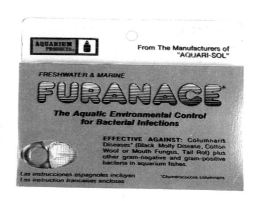

tank. Repeat this at not less than ten minute intervals until the bag is mostly tank water—about three changes at least. Meanwhile watch how the other fishes behave. If there are signs of aggression, keep the fish in its bag until they die down, but remember not to let it suffocate; keep on with the water changes or put in an airstone. Finally submerge each bag and allow the newcomer to swim out into the aquarium. Then watch to see that it appears calm and is not attacked. If it is attacked, try to judge the severity and be ready to remove it if necessary. Mild bickering without damage is permissible, but tearing of fins or similar damage is not.

OTHER THAN FISHES

There are not many other creatures suitable for inclusion in the fish tank. Most insects are likely either to eat a small fish or be eaten by it. Crayfish are safe with most fishes, but

Some fishes, including many bettas, are seclusive fish. Know a fish's behavior characteristics, so as to be able to perceive illness-suggesting behaviors. Pictured is *Betta macrostoma*.

Snails are probably the most frequently included freshwater non-fish creatures. Many have interesting characteristics and are well worth inclusion into your tank. Pictured is the gold snail, *Pomacea* sp.

will be attacked by some; turtles are safe with larger fishes but will eat small ones. Aquarium-bred snails should not carry any disease, but wild-caught ones are dangerous. Most species are vegetarians but leave healthy plants alone. Several species of *Limnaea*, whelk-like snails, are available and some eat decaying flesh and may do a useful job. The red snails, *Bulinus australianus* (the Australian red snail) and the red variety of *Planorbis corneus* (the ramshorn snail) are both attractive. The Malayan snail, *Melanoides tuberculata*, is a small burrowing snail that eats anything and helps to keep the gravel clean. It emerges in the dark and may be culled then, as it is a rapid breeder.

Newts, salamanders, and the axolotl can be kept in a

Although newts are not commonly kept with fishes in an aquarium, and for good reason, they are fascinating creatures and may very well be worth the establishing of a separate tank for them. This is a Hong Kong newt (*Paramesotriton hongkongensis*).

tropical tank, but only the latter is happy if kept in water all the time. The others like to emerge onto land out of the breeding season. However, trials have shown that they can be acclimatized in some cases to remain aquatic as long as they can climb out onto a plant or ledge when they feel like it.

PERIODIC MAINTENANCE

As a general guide, the following daily, weekly, etc., checks and procedures should be undertaken:

DAILY. Look at the thermometer and at *all* the fishes. See that all the equipment is working properly. Feed lightly morning and evening.

WEEKLY. Clean the front glass and make up for evaporation. See if the box filter needs the top mat renewed; the rest should be OK.

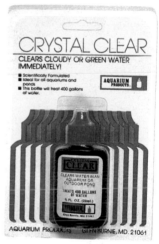

Proper maintenance will in most cases prevent any diseases from showing up in your tank; yet, if they do, rest assured that there is a remedy to suit your emergency—check your local pet shop.

MONTHLY. Change about 20–25% of the water, syphoning off mulm. Replace with conditioned water at the right temperature. Thin out the plant growth and replant bunched plants where necessary. Check the pH and correct if needed.

QUARTERLY. Renew the carbon filter. Check over all equipment and replace clogged airstones. Tighten all airline connections. Stir up the surface gravel where possible and syphon off the debris that has accumulated with not more than one-third of the gravel itself removed. Never completely change the gravel unless taking down the aquarium entirely to start up again as new.

Plants perform a very important function in the aquarium besides looking decorative. They absorb waste products and do not normally need fertilizing, as the fishes provide their needs. They grow and work for their living only if adequately lit. Adequate lighting for one species may not be enough for another, so that it pays

PLANTS

to be acquainted with the needs of various types of plants. Naturally, the fast growers that usually need good illumination contribute most to the health of the tank. If you like plants, get a good aquarium plant book.

In sufficient light, plants mop up carbon dioxide and release oxygen. This process of *photosynthesis* involves the manufacture of simple sugars by combining carbon dioxide with water; later on the sugars are built up into more complex compounds. It counters the effects of *respiration* that in both plants and animals uses up oxygen and releases carbon dioxide. In the dark, only respiration occurs, and so the plants then join the fishes in depleting the water of oxygen.

Plants also give shelter to the fishes and are eaten by some of them. In addition, they often serve to receive eggs when the fishes are spawning. It is therefore very useful to include them and is best to use real plants, not plastic ones. The healthy growth of plants is a constant measure of the fitness of the aquarium and a most important contribution to it.

STRAP-LEAVED PLANTS

There are two important *genera* (groups of species) of this type of plant, *Sagittaria* and *Vallisneria*. They are usually employed as background species, planted at the rear and perhaps the sides of the aquarium.

FACING PAGE: In addition to absorbing wastes and producing oxygen, plants also provide hiding places for chased fish and fish fry. The fish finding shelter here are *Nannostomus marginatus*.

Sagittaria subulata, from the eastern U.S.A., comes in several varieties and is a popular species, propagating rapidly in good light by runners that produce rows of young plants. The variety S. sublata var. gracillima has narrow, bright green leaves about ¼" (½ cm) wide at most and up to three ft (90 cm) long. In a small tank it may need cropping to avoid a tangle at the top. The variety kurziana or japonica is similar, but has wider leaves, about ⅗" (1½ cm) across. The variety subulata is a dwarf, at most 4" (10 cm) in length and suitable for more forward planting.

Another species, S. graminea, also offers several varieties, but is best avoided as it tends to break surface and form the arrow-shaped leaves from which the genus is named (arrowhead). It is also intolerant of hard water.

Vallisneria americana is from the southern U.S.A. It is intolerant of cold or hard water, but a very popular tropical plant. The leaves are tightly coiled, and grow to only 12" (30 cm) and are very attractive. It is often sold as V. torta.

In addition to the many live plants available, there is a wide variety of plastic plants to choose from. If you wish to avoid the maintenance required by live plants, plastic plants may be for you.

This is an *Egeria densa*. It is a profuse grower and requires a high tank. In a smaller tank it will require frequent trimmings; these clippings can be replanted or left floating on the water surface, to thereby provide cover for fry or bubblenests.

V. spiralis does not have particularly spiral leaves, as the name refers to the flower stem. It grows to several feet long and is not to be recommended.

V. asiastica, in contrast, does have nicely coiled, bright green leaves and is very attractive. However, it grows quite slowly and does not contribute as much as *V. americana* to the health of the aquarium. All *Vallisneria* species propagate by runners, as do all *Sagittaria* species.

BUNCHED PLANTS

Bunched plants are made to appear so by thrusting several short stems into the gravel, where they form roots and grow. Many species grow too long and the lower parts deteriorate, so it is usual to pinch them off and replant short pieces.

Elodea nutalli is found in Europe but originated from North America. Thrust into the gravel, it grows about 5" (12½ cm) and has whorls of small ¼–½" (½–1 cm) leaves that curl downward and are most attractive.

Egeria densa from South America (but now found elsewhere) looks much the same as *Elodea,* but grows very long and has to be pinched off and frequently replanted.

Hygrophila polysperma is a rapidly growing plant from India with long stems bearing light green pairs of leaves up to 2" x ½" (5 cm x 1 cm). *H. corymbosa,* from Malaya, is a similar but much larger plant. *H. difformis,* water wisteria, from the East, has finely divided leaves and looks very elegant, but does not flourish in hard water or bright light.

Ludwigia arcuata, from eastern U.S.A., has reddish stems and emerald green leaves about 1" x ⅕" (2½ x ½ cm) and likes bright light. There are various other *Ludwigia* species and hybrids, all rather alike so that it is difficult to be sure of what you are buying, but they are all good aquarium plants.

Myriophyllum aquaticum, parrot feather, from the Americas originally but now everywhere, has finely divided light green leaves in whorls on long stems. A favorite pond species, but it prefers hard, alkaline water. Worth a try in the aquarium, as are many other *Myriophyllum* species, some with attractive reddish foliage.

Limnophila aquatica, from India and Sri Lanka, commonly sold as *Ambulia,* is a very attractive plant with finely divided leaves. *L. sessiliflora,* from Asia in general, is the usual plant on sale, but should be avoided as it becomes spidery and pale in good light. *L. aromatica,* also from Asia, has undivided leaves and likes a good light.

Cabomba carolineana is an American plant that is brittle and easily damaged, but pretty if carefully handled. It comes in various varieties, most with closely spaced, finely divided, reddish to bright green leaves up to 3" (7½ cm) long. It is often sold as *C. aquatica.*

Ceratophyllum demersum, hornwort, worldwide in distribution, is really a coldwater plant and best avoided. It has

This is *Limnophila aquatica*; it comes from Asia, is attractive, and likes good lighting.

whorls of very brittle two-pronged leaves. *C. submersum* has three-pronged leaves and is equally unsuitable.

OTHER PLANTS

The genus *Aponogeton,* from Asia, Africa, and Australia, offers many species and hybrids. Many plants on offer are sold as species but are really hybrids that look like a particular species but are better adapted to the aquarium. They prefer soft water in general.

A. crispus has wavy-edged leaves up to 12″ x 1″ (30 x 2½ cm), reddish and very attractive. Various hybrids generally have wider, green leaves. Unusually, all tolerate hard water and like bright light.

A. elongatus, from Australia, is a large plant with long petioles (leaf stems) and leaves up to 15″ (37 cm) in length, green to reddish in color. Hybrids with *A. ulvaceus* are common.

A. *ulvaceus* is another large plant, like A. *elongatus* a bit too large for many aquaria. It has long bright green leaves up to 20″ (50 cm) on long petioles and is a beautiful plant. It comes from Madagascar.

A. *undulatus* from Malaya has tuberous roots from which new plants develop and has green crimped leaves up to 15″ (37 cm) long. Most plants sold as the species are hybrids.

A. *madagascariensis,* the Madagascar lace plant, is a large, touchy plant that lasts only a season and needs frequent changes of soft, acid water. The leaves have holes between the veins and look very showy when carefully tended. It is not a plant for beginners.

The genus *Echindorus* includes the well-known Amazon sword plants among many aquarium species, ranging from dwarf to huge varieties.

E. *amazonicus* from Brazil, the small-leaved Amazon sword plant, has short-stemmed lance-shaped leaves about 6″ (15 cm) long. It likes high temperatures above 77°F (26°C), hard

Bacopa monniera is a light-loving tropical plant that grows well, emersed as well as submersed.

Amazon swordplants do well at a range of temperatures under a range of water conditions. In short, they are rather hardy plants; they do best in medium-hard water.

water, and propagates by runners. It will tolerate quite soft water and can be grown in the usual community tank. A related and similar plant, *E. parviflorus,* grows up to 50 leaves with red-brown veins and is very showy indeed.

E. berteroi from southern U.S.A. and Central America is another good aquarium plant with bright green leaves that start grass-like in shape, become oval and then heart-shaped as they grow.

E. maior from Brazil looks like an *Aponogeton,* with light green crinkly leaves. It adapts to bright or shady conditions and is a very handsome plant.

E. quadricostatus var. *xinguensis,* the dwarf Amazon sword plant, has green leaves up to 6" x ½" (15 x 1 cm). A popular plant, it grows in soft or hard water over a temperature range of 60°–85°F (15°–30°C) and reproduces rapidly by runners. It must have been named prior to the discovery of *E. terellus*!

E. terellus, from the southern U.S.A. and Paraguay, grows less than 2" (5 cm) high. It is another rapid reproducer,

Cryptocoryne johoriensis; it's a lustrous but often hard to keep plant.

liking a temperature of 70°–85°F (21°–30°C).

The genus *Cryptocoryne* supplies another large range of aquarium plants; most of them are demanding but many are quite beautiful. The water must usually be mildly acid, around pH 6.5, soft and clean. A sandy and peaty substrate with mulm around the roots is preferred, and a dim light. The temperature should not vary much, but may be between 70°–85°F (21°–30°C).

C. affinis from Malaysia is a fast growing plant for a "crypt" and has leaves 4″–6″ (10–15 cm) long, spear-shaped, emerald green above and purple below, on similar length petioles. Reproduction is by runners and there are often lily-like underwater flowers—quite unusual.

C. axelrodii (also incorrectly called *C. willisii* and *C. undulata)* from Sri Lanka has petioles and leaves both about 4″ (10 cm) long, olive green above and reddish below. A popular plant that tolerates medium hard water.

C. becketii, from Sri Lanka, is another tough, popular plant with long petioles and short, 3″ (7½ cm) leaves, olive brown above and pink or purple below.

C. nevillii, from Sri Lanka, is available in two forms, either with dark green oval leaves 3″ x 1″ (7½ x 2½ cm) or with long, strap-shaped leaves about 4″ x ½″ (10 x 4 cm) on 6″ (15 cm) petioles. It propagates by runners.

The foregoing species are unusually tolerant plants and are to be specially recommended. Most other *Cryptocoryne* species are not for the beginner.

Ceratopteris thalictroides, water sprite, is a fern. It and *C. siliquosa* are from various parts of the tropics and both have deeply divided flat green leaves. *C. siliquosa* is even more decorative than *C. thalictroides.* They are rapid growers that form new plants on the leaves, (roots and all!) that can be separated from the parent.

FLOATING PLANTS

Most floating plants are a nuisance in the aquarium. They block the light and grow very rapidly, and some have no room to reach up into the air as they should, unless covers are omitted. However, a few species are useful as spawning media or for giving shelter to the young of livebearers.

Nitella flexilis, universal in the Northern Hemisphere, is an alga. It forms dense green mats in the water but, as it does best in hard alkaline conditions, it is of limited use.

Riccia fluitans, crystalwort, is found almost everywhere and is a liverwort that does well in soft, acid water. Masses of interlocked, multi-pronged green plants float under the water surface, each plant being an inch or so (2½ cm) in size.

Riccia fluitans is a valuable plant to have when you are breeding or when cultivating plants requiring weak lighting; this plant will form a dense mat across the surface of the tank if conditions are right.

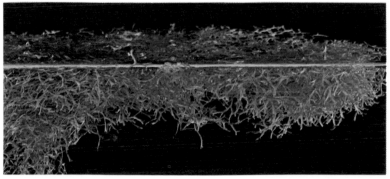

Apart from the goldfish, the first exotic species known to have been brought into Europe was the paradise fish, *Macropodus opercularis.* It was brought from China in 1868 by Mr. Simori, the French Consul at Ningpo, and was bred in 1869 by Pierre Carbonnier. Next

FISH

came a truly tropical fish, the Siamese fighting fish, *Betta splendens,* in 1874, bred in 1893,

MAINTENANCE

also in France. Then

came some of the American sunfishes, *Lepomis gibbosus* and *Ambloplites rupestris* in 1877, later several others, but not all were tropical species. It may well be that the fishes mentioned by Samuel Pepys in his famous diary (1665) as "finely marked they are being foreign" were paradise fishes, but we can only guess.

So apart from the two anabantoid fishes imported before 1880, no exotic tropicals seem to have been seen in Europe until after that date, and very few in 1900. Our hobby is certainly a new one as far as the temperate world is concerned. Before World War I, about 250 species had been imported to Europe and between the two World Wars, about the same number, perhaps another 100 by 1960, making a total of some 600 or so in all. There has been a great further expansion since then, of course. Many of the early imports were received in America either direct or via Germany, sending them over as early as the 1900s. The United Kingdom remained behind both Germany and the U.S.A., showing little interest in tropicals until 1920 or later.

PECULIARITIES OF FISHES

Many of the mistakes made by beginning aquarists

FACING PAGE: Raising healthy fishes requires a general knowledge of the anatomical and physiological differences between fishes and ourselves. Pictured is a head study of *Aequidens rivulatus.*

arise from misunderstandings about the way fishes live. Although they are vertebrates like ourselves, they are cold-blooded and respond very differently to their environment, to its temperature, to the food supply, and to the rapidity of change.

The biggest anatomical and physiological difference between fishes and ourselves and land creatures in general is the presence of gills and the absence of lungs. Otherwise, they are built on the same basic plan as we are, with a backbone, four limbs, an intestinal tract with the same organs, liver, pancreas and so forth, and with two sexes. The gills serve the same purpose as the lungs, to exchange gases with the environment, mainly to absorb oxygen and get rid of carbon dioxide. They also exchange salts with the water, whereas lungs do not deal with salts, but they do deal with water vapor.

Another big difference is the way fishes move. Although this varies from species to species, the commonest way of moving is by means of the muscular tail and its fin, using the other fins as balancing organs. Deviations from this pattern are seen in slow swimming, sometimes fast swimming as well, by using the pectoral fins that correspond to our forelimbs, or even by crawling around the bottom using these and perhaps the pelvic fins. Land animals move mainly by using all four limbs, but there are exceptions—think of snakes, for example, and man.

RESPONSE TO TEMPERATURE

Warm-blooded creatures keep their body temperature as steady as possible and respond to changes in outside temperature by changing their own metabolic activity and requirement for food. Fishes remain at about the same temperature as the water they are in, although it has been found that large, active fishes like tuna may be a few degrees above the water temperature. In addition, most tropical fishes are adapted to a rather narrow temperature range, typically 70°–85°F (21°—30°C), and respond poorly to rapid changes in temperatures, even within that range. Coldwater fishes can usually stand a much wider range of temperature, but still do not like a sudden change of more than a few degrees. In both types of fish, ab-

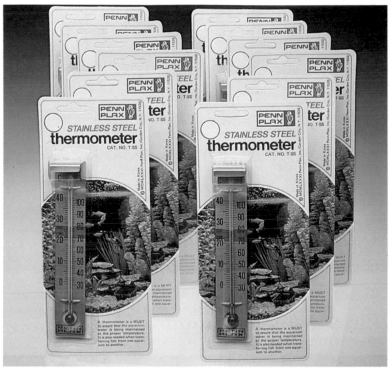

Although the range of the temperature at which most tropical fish may be kept varies some 15°F, any change within that range must be gradual, otherwise it may be an invitation for disease.

normal behavior and disease may follow a rapid change, in particular, downward.

When the external temperature rises, we tend to lose our appetite and consume less food because we do not need as much to keep our own body temperature up. When this happens to a fish, its appetite increases because its body temperature also rises and all of its chemical reactions speed up. It reacts very differently, therefore becoming more active and getting very hungry up to a limit of about 82°F (28°C), but varying with species. Then the lower oxygen content of the warmer water starts to affect it and it slows down again.

Another response to a mild rise in temperature in most adult fishes is spawning. Although many will spawn eventually without it, a rise of 3–5°F (2-3°C) triggers the reaction within a day or so. This is probably a natural reaction to seasonal changes, although they are minimal in the tropics. During

The color that your fish displays can be used as a factor in determining the health of the fish. A healthy fish displays its true colors in brilliancy, as with this *Aulonocara*.

warmer weather, the eggs will hatch more rapidly and food supplies will tend to be at their best.

An exception to the rule about guarding against sudden changes in water temperature occurs when fishes have been chilled severely. When this occurs, as with chilling in transit for example, it is better to raise the temperature quite rapidly to within the normal range. The usual flotation technique should still be used, but don't take more than a half hour over it.

RESPONSE TO FEEDING

Here is another big difference between mammalian young and fish fry or immatures. A partly starved mammal grows up skinny and miserable, but it still grows up, perhaps a bit stunted but not very much smaller than normal. A partly starved young fish just doesn't grow much. It just stays small and reasonably proportioned and may even mature sexually and breed at a fraction of the normal adult size. A good example of this was seen with some of the experiments of placing young fishes in rice paddies, usually *Tilapia* species, which tended to survive in overcrowded conditions and to remain and breed when quite tiny. Naturally, a well-grown fish cannot stand a poor diet as it is already well developed and needs adequate nourishment to maintain its tissues.

A further important difference from mammals is that fishes, as far as has been studied, are very good in comparison at making use of their food. The general rule for wild creatures and man is that only about 10% of what is eaten becomes flesh in the growing animal; some farm animals do better at 20% or 30%, but fishes achieve 50% or better. This means that what may seem to us a very meager ration is quite adequate for a fish, and that it is very easy to overfeed. Young fishes, to grow rapidly, need frequent small feeds; they cannot eat enough at one time to last them very long. Fry need practically constant feeding for normal development and without it they will remain stunted or die, or become cannibals with very few surviving.

If you are breeding fishes for sale, you will naturally want to feed the young as generously as possible and grow them large enough for sale in as short a time as possible. But if you are just keeping a tank of fishes for enjoyment, there is no point in feeding as generously as that; they will only grow rapidly and are very likely exceed the capacity of the aquarium.

Remembering that a relatively underfed fish merely grows more slowly without showing signs of undernourishment, it pays to feed adequately but not to the limit. Unless you are growing the fishes for breeding, a restricted diet may therefore be indicated, but it must be a nourishing diet, with adequate protein in particular.

OTHER PECULIARITIES

The lateral line system in fishes is possessed by no other vertebrates. It consists of a set of canals on the head, extending as a line down the body on each side. The canals lie under the skin with pores opening at the surface, filled with a viscous jelly-like substance and with bristles at the base. These detect vibrations in the water and inform a fish about its surroundings by a kind of radar and are probably the way schooling fishes act in unison. We retain a remnant of the system, in

the form of the inner ear, which detects movement as well as taking part in hearing.

The labyrinth is another peculiar organ seen in ana-bantoid fishes that use it as an auxiliary breathing apparatus. It is richly supplied with a network of blood vessels over which air gulped at the surface is passed. The fish is thus able to live in oxygen-deficient water, where the habit of building a bubble-nest keeps the eggs and fry as near to the open air as possible.

The swim bladder is an internal air-sac that may be connected to the gut; its particular function is to keep the weight of the fish about equal to that of the water it displaces so that it does not have to exert itself to stay put. Particularly

Presented here is a breeding pair of *Aphyosemion (Diapteron) cyanostictum*. One of the more fascinating aspects of the fish-keeping hobby is the witnessing of mating and courtship behavior.

when the swim bladder is isolated from the gut, it is dangerous to the fish to be suddenly hauled up from deep water. The swim bladder will expand under the reduced pressure and may burst and kill the fish. Normally, small differences in pressure are adjusted for by gas exchange with the blood, or into the gut.

REPRODUCTION

Fishes have two sexes, but the mechanism for produc-ing them is not as stable as in most higher vertebrates. Marine fishes quite often change sex as they grow up, but this is un-common in freshwater fishes. However, the genetic mechanism by which sex is determined is sometimes unstable and can be shifted experimentally from one pair of chromosomes to another, as in the guppy.

The livebearing fishes produce living young. The main group of aquarium livebearers includes the guppy, swordtail, platy, and molly. Fertilization is internal, the male possessing an organ, the gonopodium, a modified anal fin by which he places packets of spermatozoa into the female's genital aperture. One packet of spermatozoa can last for months and so the female can continue to produce young after a single fertilization, either as successive litters or a few at a time over a long period. During their stay in the mother, the young may be nourished, not only by the yolk, but by a placenta that is characteristically formed within the ovary from the pericardium.

The egglaying fishes, which means most fishes, shed eggs and spermatozoa into the water, where fertilization must usually occur quite rapidly, as the spermatozoa of those species investigated are very short-lived. The eggs are most often shed into the water and ignored, or even eaten if left in a confined space with the parents. Some species, notably the anabantoid and cichlid fishes, care for the eggs or young, building nests or guarding eggs on a leaf or rock. The anabantoids abandon the young after hatching, but the cichlids continue to care for them and do not eat them at any stage. Consult a book on fish physiology for more information.

This pair, the same pair as shown on the preceding page, is going through their courtship ritual.

FEEDING

The natural foods of many freshwater fishes have been studied in detail and the species most investigated have naturally been of commercial importance. We know that the brooktrout eats an average of 89% insects, 8% crustaceans and 3% other fishes or mollusks. This gives it 49% protein, 15% fat, and 36% carbohydrates and chitin, from the insect and crustacean integuments. The chitin is not digested.

Among the hobbyist's fishes, the majority are either carnivorous like the trout or omnivorous, eating both animal and vegetable food. The livebearers need a supply of vegetable foods, but will eat almost anything edible as well. *Characins* and *Cyprinodonts* feed like the trout if they can, but a few prefer vegetable matter. *Cyprinids* are omnivorous; Indian barbs, for instance, have been found on autopsy to have eaten algae, including diatoms, but some species also ate crustaceans. Practically all the rest of our aquarium species are carnivorous by preference; many are omnivorous by necessity, but odd species like some of the gouramis and catfishes are vegetarians.

PREPARED FOODS

The capacity of fishes to convert so much of their food to flesh means that a high protein content of the diet is strongly indicated. Experiments have shown the need for a minimum of around 45%, the warmer the water the greater the need for a high protein content. Vitamins of the B group and, for some species, vitamin C are necessary; the literature is less specific about other vitamins and it is a puzzle why the livers of some fishes store so much of vitamins A and D.

FACING PAGE: To keep your fish and aquarium healthy and clean, feed in carefully measured amounts, making sure that all of the food is eaten and that everyone gets his share. These exotic looking fish are "glass fish" (*Chanda ranga*).

Prepared foods should therefore be high in protein, preferably first class protein containing all the necessary amino acids for health. Of all the varieties, freeze-dried foods can offer the highest amounts—krill, for example, may go as high as 65% protein. Freeze-dried "plankton," which varies from krill itself to tiny crustaceans, etc., is also very good; so are bloodworms, tubifex, and brine shrimp. But none of them is suitable as a staple diet—in fact nothing is, because we don't yet know enough to offer one. Feed them frequently, but never exclusively.

Flakes of one kind or another are probably the commonest prepared food used today. They can be very good too, although the pretty colors usually mean nothing. They can contain just about the right diet for many species of fishes, predominantly animal or vegetable in make-up. However, few varieties give sufficient details for the aquarist to be sure of their suitability as the quantities of the various constituents are not given—just as with human foods! As to the other attributes of flakes, they should not be thin and crumbly, should float on the water and then gradually sink without any clouding effect. Never feed them exclusively either. For larger fishes, pelleted or granulated foods can contain more than flakes, such as tiny insects and crustaceans, fragments of plants or pieces of larger animal matter. They can be ground up and fed to small fishes as well.

Frozen foods are also very popular. They are not really good value for the money, but are good for the fishes. They

Today's hobbyists have the advantage of frozen and freeze-dried foods. They provide much the same nutrient value as live food while being more convenient, easy to store and use.

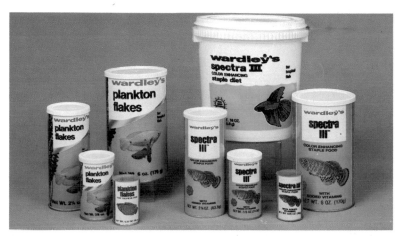

A common practice among hobbyists is to choose a fine flake food and make it their staple, supplementing it with frozen and live foods as they feel necessary.

contain a lot of water, but since they closely resemble their living counterparts, many fishes prefer them and may refuse other prepared foods. Canned foods are similar and usually cheaper.

Avoid feeding ordinary meat such as ham, beloved of European aquarists, beef heart or any other meat high in saturated fats, which fishes can poorly digest. Even fish itself has vitamin-destroying properties and is best not fed too often. Heart is toxic in large quantities and meats cause digestive upsets. Of course, fishes that feed on other fishes can take such a diet, but not the general run of insect eaters or omnivores.

LIVE FOODS

Such is the satisfactory nature of many prepared foods that the use of live foods is neglected by most of us. Yet it has recently been shown that they are capable of considerably increasing the fertility of tropical fishes and should at least be used by breeders. The same is true when feeding the young. Even in the ordinary community tank, it is wise to feed some live foods as frequently as is convenient. They are much liked by the fishes and help to keep them healthy. Most pet shops offer a variety of live foods such as tubifex, *Daphnia,* brine shrimps, white or micro worms. Some of these can be grown at home with little trouble. Get a book on live foods. It may be the best investment you ever made!

Brine shrimp are the easiest to deal with and can be fed to the fishes either as newly-hatched *nauplii* or as more adult forms. The shrimp, *Artemia salina*, lay "eggs" that can be dried and stored for several years without loss of vitality. They are really at an early stage of development, not just one-celled eggs. They may also be purchased shelled, which avoids any problems of separating the hatchlings from the empty shells.

The eggs hatch out in sea water, even in sea water diluted half and half with fresh water, or in a 2% to 3.5% solution of common salt (not table salt; that contains additives). You may use a kit bought with the eggs, or follow one of these methods for eggs in shell:

1. For small hatches, use a shallow pan holding ½–1 gallon (2–4 liters) of water and float a half teaspoon eggs per gallon carefully on the surface. Keep at 70°–80°F (21°–27°C), preferably the higher temperature, and leave for about two days. The young will hatch and swim down into the water and can be syphoned off from the floating egg shells. Wash them in fresh water and feed to small fishes or fry. The salt water can be re-used.

2. For larger hatches, use gallon bottles and fill three-quarters full. Add up to one teaspoon of eggs per bottle and aerate briskly. After two days, turn off the air and leave to settle. The shells will either float or collect on the bottom, leaving the *nauplii* swimming. Syphon off as before.

The *nauplii* can be grown if transferred to a stronger brine; that for San Francisco eggs should consist of 10 oz (280 g) of common salt, 2 oz (56 g) of Epsom salts and 1 oz (28 g) of baking soda (bicarbonate of soda) per gallon, more if you intend to use them part grown, and aerate strongly. Feed on baker's yeast, only a pinch or two, and repeat as it clears. It will take six to eight weeks at 70°F (21°C) or over to reach the adult stage.

Mikro worms are small worms related to the vinegar eel, probably *Anguillula silusiae*, and grow to about ¹⁄₁₀" (¼ cm). Their young are very small indeed and make suitable fry feed. They are cultivated in plastic boxes with about ⅕" (½ cm) layer of any breakfast cereal cooked with milk. When it is cool, add a little baker's yeast and some worms and stack wat-

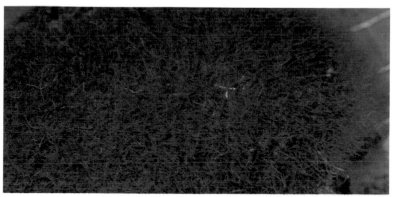

Tubifex worms are a common and very nutritious live meal; like many live foods, however, they are high in fat and must be fed in moderation.

er-soaked small sticks in tiers that stick up from the food for two or three layers, cover and keep in the dark at up to 80°F (27°C). Keep a series of cultures going and harvest the worms from the sticks and sides of the boxes.

Grindal worms and *white worms (Enchytraeus albidus)* are small round worms approximately ½" (1 cm) and 1" (2.5 cm) respectively. Both are cultivated in clean soil in plastic boxes with small pockets of any milky baby food or cooked cereal covered by a sheet of glass and then an opaque top cover or lid. The worms accumulate around the food and stick to the glass. Grindal worms like to be at 70°–75°F (21°–24°C) but white worms like it cooler.

Earthworms are of course much bigger and are fine foods for large fishes if fed whole or in pieces. For smaller fishes they can be finely chopped or even ground up if you are not squeamish. They may be stored or bred in damp leaf mold or bought in any quantities you wish.

Tubificid worms (Tubifex) are various species of worms living at the bottom of polluted streams. They occur in quantity as reddish or brown waving masses—their tails collecting oxygen. Different species are 1"–6" (2½–15 cm) long. When collected or even if bought from a petshop, they need careful cleaning, as they feed on filth. Put them in a vessel under a dripping tap and break up the masses from time to time until

they look nice and clean. Feed sparingly or they will establish themselves in the aquarium. This may *seem* good, but it isn't, as they tend to overpopulate it and deprive the fishes of oxygen. They are also too fatty for frequent use, despite being very popular with the majority of fishes.

Water fleas (Daphnia pulex) are another popular food you may collect or buy. They swarm in cool water as green or reddish masses and can be bred successfully in large vats of not less than about 50 gallons (200 liters). Feed on liver powder or dried blood. Other small crustaceans may be collected occasionally *(Moina, Diaptomus* or the larger *Asellus, Gammarus,* or *Hyallela)* and most can be bred as for *Daphnia. Cyclops* is to be avoided, as it can become a pest and is not liked by many fishes.

Mosquito larvae are another fine food and can be graded after collection with domestic kitchen sieves or strainers. They start as tiny egg rafts floating on the surface of small ponds or puddles and hatch out as equally tiny air-breathing "wrigglers," suitable for fry. In the course of the next eight or nine days, they grow to about ⅓" (1 cm) and then turn into comma-shaped pupae that soon hatch out as unwanted mosquitos. As they do not use up oxygen from the water, the larvae and pupae can be fed freely. Store them in air-tight jars in the refrigerator.

Bloodworms (Chironomus), the larvae of a gnat, are red and up to 1" (2½ cm) long, and are good for the bigger fishes. They live rather deep in the water, so be careful of collecting predators with them. The *glass worm (Chaborus)* is a similar but colorless larva from colder waters.

When collecting any live foods from the wild, it is best not to do so from ponds containing fishes, as there is always the danger of introducing diseases or parasites to the aquarium. If you happen to live near the sea, it is fine to collect from tide pools or splash pools, where saltwater mosquito larvae and small crustaceans, etc., often abound and will not be a danger. This "cross-over" feeding technique, of saltwater live foods to freshwater fishes and of freshwater live foods to marine fishes, is a very good idea where feasible, as it guards against many diseases and parasitic troubles, although not all of them.